Bruno Santi

San Lorenzo

Guide to the Laurentian complex

SANDAK

A DIVISION OF G.K. HALL & Co.

Contents

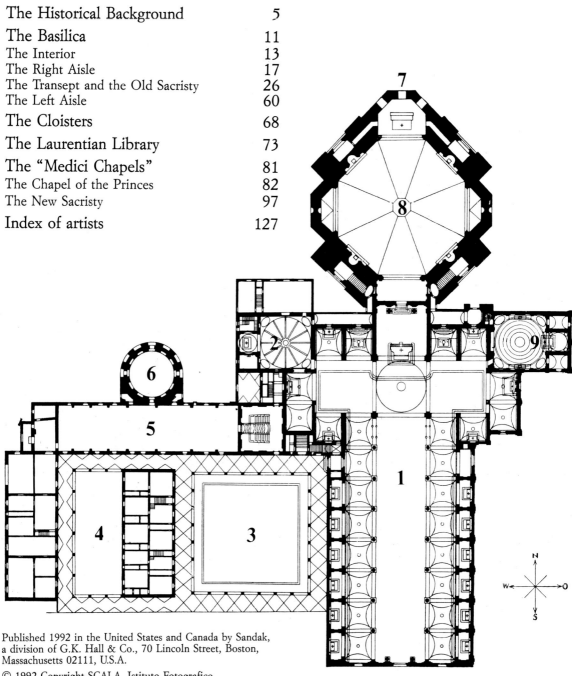

Published 1992 in the United States and Canada by Sandak, a division of G.K. Hall & Co., 70 Lincoln Street, Boston, Massachusetts 02111, U.S.A.

© 1992 Copyright SCALA, Istituto Fotografico Editoriale, Antella (Florence), and Editrice Giusti di Becocci & C., Florence
Translation: Susan Madocks Lister
Photographs: SCALA (M. Falsini and M. Sarri), except pp. 4, 35, 72c (V. Silvestri); pp. 10, 33, 84 (Soprintendenza ai Beni Artistici e Storici, Florence); pp. 79a (D. Pineider/ Laurentian Library)
Printed in Italy by Sogema Marzari, Schio (Vicenza), 1992

Legend
1 Basilica
2 Old Sacristy
3 Brunelleschi's cloister
4 Second cloister
5 Laurentian Library
6 Tribuna d'Elci or 'Rotonda'
7 Entrance to the Medici Chapels
8 Chapel of the Princes
9 New Sacristy

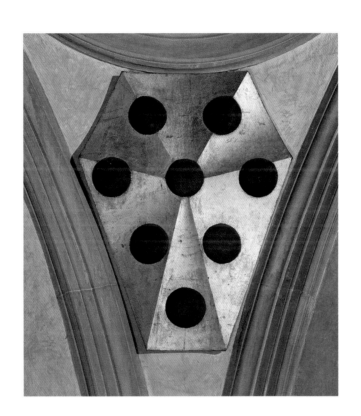

The facade of San Lorenzo   The building complex of San Lorenzo

THE HISTORICAL BACKGROUND

San Lorenzo is unparalleled among other Florentine churches in that its history is so closely interwoven with the very origins of local Christianity, with the most significant cultural and artistic renewal the city has ever known, and with the rise of the family who were the church's patrons to the pinnacle of power in Florence and subsequently in the whole of Tuscany.

Three significant reasons, then, that allow the basilica and its related buildings an exceptionally important place in that remarkable realization of architectural and artistic projects which Florence still today preserves as testimony to her age-old creative powers. And yet, whoever looks at the exterior bulk of the building gets barely a hint that within there took place the most innovative – and in some cases revolutionary – achievements in the sphere both of the figurative arts and of architecture in the whole cultural history of Florence. This is becaus the exterior has a somewhat harsh and unprepossessing look, due mainly to the rough unfinished facade and, sadly, because of the dilapidation of the stone facing and the steps which lead to the base from which the church rises – a clear sign of the neglect of the public authorities.

The history of the founding of the church is in itself remarkable. It dates back to the earliest times of the spread of Christianity in the Roman colony of *Florentia* – brought there by sparse groups from the East who came north from Rome along the ancient route of the Via Cassia.

Just outside the first city walls of Florence,

on a small area of high ground lapped by the Mugnone (before the many diversions of this stream which pushed it increasingly to the outskirts of the city) the foundations of an oratory were laid. This was dedicated to the Roman martyr Lawrence (Lorenzo) who, on 10 August 258, was atrociously put to death by being roasted alive on burning coals; his martyrdom took place during the persecution of the Christians ordered by Emperor Valerian. A somewhat curious tradition has it that a matron of Jewish origin, Giuliana, offered to finance the construction of the church were she to bear a son who would then be named after the deacon saint. The consecration of the church, which took place in 393, is also traditionally linked to an important protagonist in the history of Christianity – Ambrose, Bishop of Milan and Father of the Western Church.

St Ambrose was in the nearby town of Faenza during this period; he came to consecrate the church and to meet his confrère Zenobius, legendary 'shepherd' of the early church in Florence.

Right from the beginning, therefore, the church of San Lorenzo is connected with key figures in religious history; it superseded all other churches in importance. It was the bishop's seat and housed the remains of St Zenobius until the founding, in the eleventh century, of the new cathedral dedicated to St Reparata. A miracle occurred during the transfer of the body of the saint. While the coffin was being borne to the Cathedral, close to the Baptistery it happened to knock against a withered elm tree which prodigiously broke into leaf. Today, near the north door of the Baptistery, this charming miracle is commemorated in a marble column topped by a sapling fashioned from wrought iron.

The second phase of the building history of San Lorenzo began in 1045, under Bishop Gerard of Burgundy, continuing until 20 January 1060 when it was reconsecrated by this same prelate who had in the meantime be-

San Lorenzo with Baccio
Bandinelli's statue of *Giovanni dalle
Bande Nere*

The early medieval appearance of
San Lorenzo in a drawing in the
codex of Florentine churches
illustrated by Marco Rustici.
Library of the 'Seminario Maggiore',
Florence

come Pope Nicholas II. The appearance of
the early medieval church is recorded in a
miniature dedicated to San Lorenzo in the
codex of Florentine churches compiled and
illustrated by Marco Rustici in 1425 and now
preserved in the library of the 'Seminario
Maggiore' of Florence.

The involvement of the Medici family in
the history of San Lorenzo coincides with the
third phase of the construction of the church.
It was Giovanni di Averado de' Medici called
Giovanni "di Bicci" who, in 1418, undertook
to radically renovate its architecture.

The project was entrusted to the most
gifted representative of the progressive movement in the visual arts in Florence – Filippo
Brunelleschi. The first part of the church to
be built in the new style was the sacristy, or

rather, the chapel dedicated to the patron
saint of Giovanni "di Bicci", John the Evangelist, and which was to serve as a family tomb
for the patron and his wife Piccarda Bueri.
The sacristy was already complete at the time
of Giovanni's death in 1429. His son Cosimo
undertook, in his turn, to complete the building of the church despite the fact that he
himself and Brunelleschi (who had been re-
confirmed in his appointment) were involved
in other architectural projects: Cosimo in that
of the new family palace which was intended
to face the piazza in front of San Lorenzo,
Brunelleschi in the construction of the Cathedral dome. And so work progressed slowly
on the patronal church of the Medici family
who had now become the real rulers of the
city and its republican institutions. But the

7

prominence of the patrons and the importance of the church were such that already in 1459 the Sienese Pope Pius II Piccolomini had conferred on San Lorenzo the honour of a supreme collegiate church. Even before this, in memory of its great importance in former times, a chapter of canons operated there as in a cathedral.

Filippo Brunelleschi died in 1446 while San Lorenzo was still under construction. His place was taken by his pupil Antonio di Manetto Ciaccheri who was also Brunelleschi's biographer. It was he who Vasari blamed for the supposed "errors" in the final building of San Lorenzo. It is more plausible to consider Manetti's work as being interpretative or maybe trivializing compared to the original Brunelleschian project.

In any event, the work went ahead and in 1461 the High Altar was consecrated. Cosimo the Elder died in 1464 and was buried beneath the presbytery of the church; his tomb is within the pier which supports it – a symbolic monument to the man who had asserted the supremacy of his own family in the city. And it was here, on his tomb, that Cosimo was accorded the title, which falls somewhere between the humanistic and the courtly: "Pater Patriae". With Cosimo's son Piero, called "the Gouty", the basilica became definitively something of a family church. In fact Piero obtained the prerogative, in 1465, to assign to important families of the San Lorenzo quarter those chapels which had not yet been built. From this point on the Medici, through their various echelons of power, considered San Lorenzo as their mausoleum and the focal point of their art patronage. Following in the footsteps of their predecessors they continued to employ the very best artistic talent the city had to offer. The elevation of the family, initiated by Giovanni di Bicci, was continued with the two Medici popes, Leo X and Clement VII. The former intended to transform the church into something of a dynastic mausoleum with the commissioning from Michelangelo of the "New" Sacristy. This was a funerary chapel dedicated to the two "Magnifici", Lorenzo and Giuliano, respectively father and uncle of Pope Leo X, and the two "Dukes" Lorenzo of Urbino and Giuliano of Nemours, respectively grandson and son of Lorenzo the Magnificent. Under Leo X Michelangelo was also instructed to design a new facade for the basilica. From Pope Clement VII he received the commission to design what is known today as the Medicean-Laurentian Library (1524-1559) which commemorates the cultural interests of the Medici family.

Once they became grandukes, beginning with Cosimo I, the Medici initiated that real celebratory repository of their absolute power: the "Cappella dei Principi" (Chapel of the Princes), an opulent structure crowned by an immense dome which, in the panorama of Florence, is second only to the triumphant cupola of the Cathedral. It was intended that the chapel should display the granducal tombs in a magnificent setting of inlaid polychromatic marbles and semi-precious stones.

The inglorious extinction of the dynasty with the death of Gian Gastone in 1737 left the grandiose projects incomplete. The last of the Medici, the Electress Palatine Anna Maria Lodovica was, however, not deficient in concerning herself with the basilica which had been so dear to her forefathers. It was she who commissioned both the bell-tower, carried out with airy eighteenth century elegance by Ferdinando Ruggieri in 1740, and the frescoes in the dome of the church, above the presbytery, painted by Vincenzo Meucci in 1742.

These were the last projects carried out by the Medici family for their patronal church. San Lorenzo had also been the setting for the obsequies of its patrons and those European monarchs related to them. The temporary decorations adorning the church on those occasions were of a transitory splendour yet they were devised with that same quality of execution dedicated to the architecture of the church itself. The unfinished state of the Medici mausoleum is singularly linked with the dashed hopes brought by their failure to be recognized as Kings of Tuscany which Cosimo III in particular had sought, lavishing diplomatic effort and substantial sums of money on this aspiration. Their successors, the House of Hapsburg-Lorraine, continued to consider San Lorenzo as the dynastic church; they buried those family members who had died in Florence in their simple and

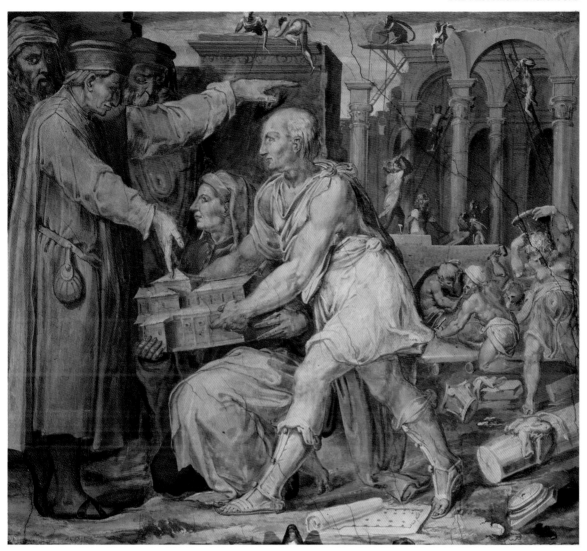

Giorgio Vasari and Marco da Faenza
Brunelleschi and Ghiberti showing Cosimo the Elder the
model for the church of San Lorenzo.
Palazzo Vecchio, Sala di Cosimo il Vecchio

unobstrusive family Crypt. They wished to complete the decoration of the dome of the Chapel of the Princes with frescoes by Pietro Benvenuti (1826-1834). This was done not in a spirit of celebratory ostentation but with a diligence befitting those who had received the inheritance of their munificent predecessors.

This, then, saw the conclusion of the architectural and decorative work on San Lorenzo and its associated buildings. Notwithstanding a certain feeling of regret for those parts of the basilica left incomplete as a result of the vicissitudes of history, it is undeniable that San Lorenzo offers the visitor a rich patrimony of architectural and artistic experience among the most significant not only in the city of Florence but in the whole field of human creativity. The inexhaustible attention dedicated to the church by a single family through the centuries, its more than a thousand years of history, the numerous works of art it contains – classic examples of the very highest expression of Florentine artistic genius – all these things not only engage the attention of the crowds of people who daily visit San Lorenzo but they also make of the church a symbol of the Renaissance period for which the city is universally famous.

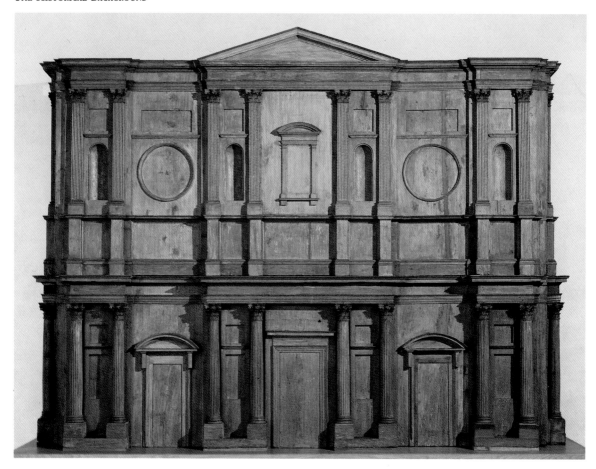

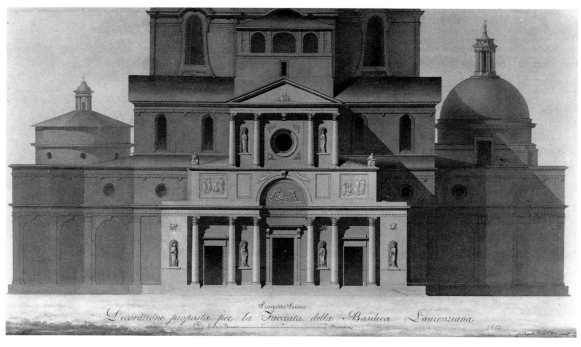

Wooden model for the facade of San Lorenzo
designed by Michelangelo.
Casa Buonarroti

Nineteenth century drawing for the facade of the
church by the architect Pasquale Poccianti.
Prints and Drawings Department, Uffizi

THE BASILICA

Looking at the church from that corner of the piazza which is dominated by the bulk of Michelozzo's Medici Palace, the facade of San Lorenzo appears severe and stony, rising from the steps below which the market stalls, with their awnings, clutter up the side of the church and which continue along the Via dell'Ariento as far as the central market – the centre of a lively working-class quarter of the city. This stone exterior – punctuated by three entrances, today protected by iron gates, and furrowed horizontally by the keyed brickwork prepared for a facing project which was never realized – was the focus of the projects of great architects – Raphael, Giuliano da Sangallo, Pasquale Poccianti – who planned to give a perfect finish and sobre elegance to the front of Brunelleschi's church. At the beginning of this tortured building history the figure of Pope Leo X features once more, none more concerned than he with the fortunes of the family church. According to Vasari the pope announced in Rome a competition for the facade design which Raphael, Baccio d'Agnolo, Andrea and Jacopo Sansovino entered joined subsequently by Michelangelo who came nearest to the completion of the project. Even if it was Jacopo Sansovino whose ideas were actually carried out in a wooden model made by Baccio d'Agnolo, it was the latter who, together with Michelangelo, received the formal commission for the facade in October 1517. They were busy on the project until 1520 when, to Michelangelo's intense disappointment, the contract was rescinded. All that remains is a wooden model, in the Casa Buonarroti, of uncertain attribution but faithful to Michelangelo's designs. It shows for the first time that "the facade is no longer a reflection of the cross-section of a church, as it is in Romanesque architecture; it already forms an independent decorative part of the building... Michelangelo was the first to assign this autonomy to the facade of a church" (Tolnay).

The seventeenth and eighteenth centuries saw no new projects for the facade of San Lorenzo. Perhaps the resources of the granducal family were all reserved for the construction of the Chapel of the Princes and they preferred to neglect the exterior of the basilica in favour of the completion of the Medici mausoleum with sumptuous inlays of coloured stones.

It was Granduke Leopold II of Lorraine who took up the cause again by entrusting the problem of the facade to the Neoclassical architect Pasquale Poccianti who had already worked on the granducal residence, the Pitti Palace, and the villa of Poggio Imperiale. Beginning in 1837 three proposals were put forward, all unrealized; they serve to document once more the difficulty of uniting the prestigious architecture of Brunelleschi and Michelangelo with the laudable efforts of the painstaking but ultimately ineffective nineteenth century style. And despite a further attempt on the part of Lorenzo Urbani in 1876 – after the unification of Italy – San Lorenzo's rough facade is eloquent testimony to the futile efforts of successive centuries to contribute on the same high level as the remarkable creations of the early and late Renaissance.

The right side of the church with the bell-tower and
the domes of the New Sacristy and the Chapel of the
Princes

The Interior

For the visitor entering the basilica the first impression is without doubt that of "a strong feeling of lucid contemplation and of refined harmony" (Berti).

The articulation of the space arrived at by the three spacious aisles of the naves, with the serene repetition of the arches (springing not directly from the capitals but from the cornices of the high impost blocks) which carry the eye towards the east end, appears at first sight (and certainly seemed so in the fifteenth century) as something entirely novel. Romanesque solidity and Gothic verticality are reconciled in a complete and harmonious conquest of space. The side chapels – framed by pilasters, with arched entrances and raised above the floor by three steps – create additional spaces in the walls of the church. The half-light of the chapels is relieved by the circular windows inserted into the lunettes above; these are connected by domed vaults to the central nave. High, arched windows, diffusing a steady, soft light open up from the cornice. The latter guides the perspective vista of the arches towards the transept, its limits defined by a double triumphal arch and topped by a cupola. Even the coffered ceiling is drawn into a calculated perspective scheme. Embellished with two gilded Medici coats of arms it gives the impression of a grand audience chamber rather than an ecclesiastical setting.

But the religious character of the building finds confirmation in the colonnade (inspired not so much by Roman antiquity as by the peaceful expressiveness of Early Christian churches) which draws the eye towards the sacred focal point of the church – the High Altar. The decoration of the arcade was carried out by the workshops of Antonio Rossellino and Pagno di Lapo Portigiani in around 1460. This repertoire of ornamental motifs includes the Corinthian capitals, the impost blocks carved with the grill – symbol of St Lawrence – and cherubs heads; the laurel garlands outlining the arches and the wreathed mouldings which decorate their undersides. The Renaissance style additions, carried out by Giuseppe Baccani in 1860, which completed the chancel and provided the chapels with rigorously identical altars, contribute to the impression of extraordinary homogeneity of the church.

More than most religious buildings in Florence San Lorenzo has retained intact both its structure and its wealth of works of art. Even the chromatic interplay between the grey sandstone elements and the white stucco emphasises the impression of formal equilibrium and harmony conjured up by a contemplation of the basilica's interior.

The inner facade, despite its obvious Brunelleschian style, was designed by Michelangelo between 1531-1532; this is made clear by the only extravagant element in the severe architecture, the Medici coat of arms inserted above the arch of the central portal (although it is the oval "stemma" with the cross of the House of Savoy which still dominates the internal facade – a reminder of the princely destiny of the church). This tribune was built to house the church's abundance of saintly relics which were displayed to the faithful from the balcony in front of the three small doors. The latter, clearly inspired by Brunelleschian models, are also reminiscent of the Florentine Romanesque style; it is enough to compare them with the windows on the facade of the Badia Fiesolana.

The centuries-old history of San Lorenzo has allowed for a rich accumulation of numerous examples of sacred art from every period. Some of these are considered to rank among the very highest artistic accomplishments of the Florentine school. Despite the somewhat banal, mock-Renaissance altars, carried out in the Romantic period, despite the displacement and substitution of paintings (some have even been moved to completely different settings, although remaining within the Laurentian complex) the pictorial and sculptural endowment of San Lorenzo boasts a significant number of very well-known artists.

Beginning from the right, we will trace the placement of these works around the church.

The interior of the church showing the inner facade
designed by Michelangelo

The interior looking towards the High Altar

Rosso Fiorentino
Marriage of the Virgin

The Right Aisle

The first chapel, which once belonged to the Medici family, is dedicated to the Visitation and now has as its altarpiece a large *Martyrdom of St Sebastian* (c 1580-1590) by Jacopo Chimenti called "L'Empoli". This was formerly in the last chapel of the left-hand aisle – dedicated to St Sebastian. This painter was involved in the post-Mannerist revival of Florentine painting and the new informal naturalism is obvious, not only in the treatment of the figures, but also in the inclusion into the composition of Alberti's domed "tribuna" of the church of Santissima Annunziata – very familiar to the Florentines.

In the second chapel (which belonged to the Ginori family and was dedicated to the Betrothal of the Virgin) the altarpiece is the glowing panel of the *Marriage of the Virgin*, a work of the capricious and unorthodox painter Rosso Fiorentino. Shot colours, crumpled and fragmented drapery, unnatural poses – the whole repertoire of Rosso is unfolded in this painting (although less dazzling than his other works) executed for Carlo Ginori in 1523. A nineteenth century inscrip-

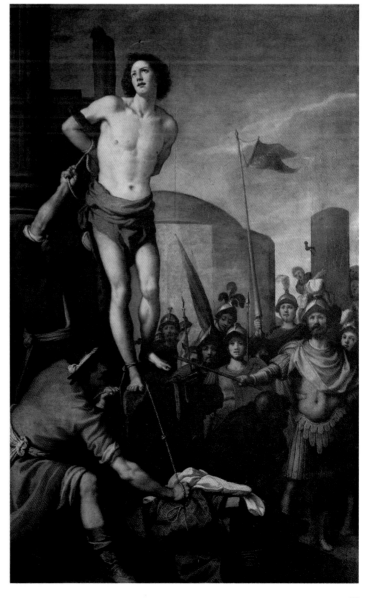

Jacopo Chimenti called "l'Empoli"
Martyrdom of St. Sebastian

Niccolò Lapi
St. Lawrence among the Souls of Purgatory

Fourteenth century
Sepulchral slab of Francesco Landini

tion commemorates three musicians, members of the Chapter of the basilica: Francesco Corteccia, Luca Bati and Marco da Gagliano, who composed madrigals and motets at the courts of Eleonora of Toledo and Anne of Austria. On the left-hand wall is a sepulchral slab with the effigy of the musician Francesco Landino called "the Blind Man of the Organs" who died in 1397.

In the third chapel, formerly belonging to the Inghirami family and dedicated to St Lawrence, the altarpiece is by Niccolò Lapi (1661-1732) depicting *St Lawrence among the Souls of Purgatory.*

The following altar, belonging to the Martelli family and dedicated to St Sigismund, contains a panel of the *Assumption of the Virgin*, a restrained work by Michele di Ridolfo del Ghirlandaio (c 1572). The fifth chapel (formerly of the Ginori family), is dedicated to St Jerome and has a large canvas – now much darkened – depicting the *Crucifixion with St Jerome, St Francis and Mary Magdalene*, a seventeenth century work at-

Michele di Ridolfo
del Ghirlandaio
*Assumption of the
Virgin*

tributed to Ottaviano Dandini.

The altarpiece of the sixth chapel (formerly of the Medici family) is an *Adoration of the Magi* by Girolamo Macchietti (c 1535-1592); painted in vivid colours, its composition is typical of early Florentine Mannerism.

Attached to the wall next to this chapel is Desiderio da Settignano's marble *Tabernacle of the Sacrament* (c 1461). Moved to this position after the Second World War, it was formerly in the Chapel of the Sacrament – to the far right of the transept. It ranks among the

most well-known and celebrated of the sculptor's works, because of the gracefulness of some of the figures and the calm dramatic force of the depiction of the *Pietà* in the base. The high tabernacle is flanked by a pair of candle-bearing angels and framed by pilasters decorated with a candelabra motif. These, together with the delicate frieze above, consisting of cherubs' head, palmettes, vegetative garlands and cornucopia, carved in very low relief, enclose an illusionary church interior rendered in perspective with a barrel-vaulted,

Desiderio da Settignano
Tabernacle of the Sacrament and detail

Detail of the *Pietà* from Desiderio da Settignano's *Tabernacle of the Sacrament*

coffered ceiling; adoring angels emerge from this setting, turning towards the small door in the background. (The absurdity of the current placing of the tabernacle is brought out by the sight of the wall framed by this door; a totally misleading impression for a tabernacle intended to enshrine the Eucharist). In the small lunette above the door God the Father is depicted blessing. It has been noted by Parronchi that the tabernacle derives from the setting of Masaccio's *Trinity* and becomes, in its turn, a model for a number of fifteenth century Florentine church ornaments of similar type. On the other hand, the Masaccio composition is never cited in painting.

On the lunette of the tabernacle, between two adoring angels, a Christ Child stands in benediction over a chalice, clasping in his left hand the symbols of the Passion – the crown of thorns and the nails – now much damaged. There are numerous derivations from this figure, too; its echoes are felt even beyond the Renaissance period.

In front of the *Tabernacle of the Sacrament* stands Donatello's much celebrated *Pulpit* which, like its pendant opposite, is supported by Ionic columns – a late sixteenth-century arrangement (1558-1565). Here the sculptor demonstrates that other complexion of the

Florentine Renaissance – the expressionistic and dramatic. Left unfinished in 1464, two years before Donatello's death, the work was completed in the seventeenth century with the addition of bronzed wood panels (1616-1634). Some scholars, like Becherucci, believe that the bronze reliefs were destined for another setting (perhaps the base of the High Altar) and that they were only assembled as pulpits at the dates indicated above.

The reliefs on the right *Pulpit* are enclosed, then, by architectural frames and they depict: the *Martyrdom of St Lawrence* (possibly a collaborative effort between Donatello and his pupil Bertoldo di Giovanni); the figure of *St Luke* and the scene of the *Mocking of Christ* (both wooden additions of the seventeenth century). Then the *Maries at the Sepulchre, Christ in Limbo,* and the shocking and tragic depiction of the *Resurrection* with Christ emerging from his tomb still swathed in his winding sheet; then the *Ascension* and *Pentecost* which reveal the collaboration of Donatello's Venetian follower Bellano. The decorative repertoire is unusual: vases, putti and centaurs. Between two of these appears Donatello's signature.

Donatello
Right *Pulpit*

Details from Donatello's *Pulpit* showing the
Martyrdom of St. Lawrence and *Christ in Limbo*

Detail from Donatello's *Pulpit* showing the
Resurrection of Christ

The Transept and the Old Sacristy

The chapel to the right, before the end of the transept, is dedicated to St Julian and came under the patronage of the Corsi family. It now contains – on the right – a fragment of a sarcophagus surmounted by a detached fresco of the graceful *Madonna dei Canonici* (*Madonna of the Canons*), attributed to Niccolò di Tommaso and therefore of the Florentine school of the second half of the fourteenth century. Following its restoration in 1972, Antonio Pollaiolo's cork-oak *Crucifix* was installed on the altar. It is a vigorously modelled work of dramatic effect. On the left wall a *Roman Sarcophagus* contains the remains of the Danish physician Niklaas Stensen (Niccolo Stenone). Born a Lutheran he converted to Catholicism and entered the Society of Jesus.

At the end of the crossing is the Chapel of the Sacrament. On either side of its entrance arch hang two late sixteenth century paintings: a *Crucifixion* and a *St Zenobius*, the latter attributed to Fabrizio Boschi. Above the Baroque altar is a large seventeenth century *Crucifix* in the style of Ferdinando Tacca. Inside the chapel, on the right, is the *Funerary Monument to Caroline of Saxony* (d. 1832) first wife of Leopold II; the tomb is one of the last productions in *pietre dure* (inlays of semi-precious stone) carried out by the Opificio delle Pietre Dure for the rulers of Tuscany. On the left wall is a late fifteenth century panel painting attributable to a follower of Domenico Ghirlandaio depicting the *Nativity with St Mark and St Francis*.

The first chapel in the right transept belonged to the Ridolfi family and is dedicated to St Bernard. It contains the *Funerary Monument to the Aretine Painter Pietro Benvenuti* who frescoed the vault of the Chapel of the Princes dome; the neoclassical style tomb was carried out by Aristodemo Costoli in 1852. On the altar, a late eighteenth century canvas of the *Education of the Virgin*, painted with almost Anglo-Saxon intimism; the artist is unknown. On the left wall is a *Monument to the Goldsmith Bernardo Cennini* (he collaborated on the decoration of the silver altar of the Florentine baptistery of San Giovanni). He was also a printer (in 1471 he published in Florence Virgil's *Bucolics*) and adopted as his publishing motto *Florentinis ingeniis nil ardui est* ("Nothing is difficult for Florentine men of genius"). This is inscribed on his centotaph which is the work of Leopoldo Costoli (1871).

The following chapel (formerly of the Della Stufa family) has, on the left wall, a long Latin inscription, dating to the eighteenth century. This summarises the history of the church and commemorates the 1712 ceremony of reconsecration which was attended by Granduke Cosimo III and the Florentine Archbishop Tommaso Bonaventura della Gherardesca.

The chancel – as is obvious – came under the patronage of the Medici family and in the floor of the crossing, in front of the altar, a remarkable polychromed *Memorial Slab* honours Cosimo the Elder. It consists of a large square with three smaller squares containing bronze grilles centred on three sides. Each corner is embellished with the Medici coat of arms and, at the centre, a geometric design is made up of an interplay of white marble, green serpentine and porphyry. This unusual memorial marks the spot where Cosimo is buried in the crypt below or, to be exact, within the pier which supports the crossing of the basilica. This reference to Cosimo is made explicit in the inscription which nominates him by his famous title: "Pater Patriae". Believed to be the work of Verrocchio (1467), this memorial is one of the most original creations of the Florentine Quattrocento despite the damage done to it in 1495 and 1517 – the years of the temporary expulsions of the Medici family from the city. Drawing inspiration as it does from the polychromatic compositions of Tuscan Romanesque, this work anticipates the great flourishing of the art of inlaid *pietre dure* (otherwise known as Florentine mosaic) in the centuries to come.

The High Altar was carried out by the Opificio delle Pietre Dure in 1787, on a de-

View of the transept seen from the Chapel of the
Relics

Antonio Pollaiolo
Crucifix

Niccolò di Tommaso (attrib.)
Madonna dei Canonici

School of Domenico Ghirlandaio
Nativity with Saints Mark and Francis

Roman sarcophagus used as the tomb of Niccolò Stenone

sign by Gaspare Maria Paoletti. Very ornately framed panels depicting the *Sacrifice of Isaac* and the *Gathering of Manna* were inserted. These were designed by Poccetti and, presumably, Cigoli, for the projected ciborium for the altar of the Granducal mausoleum – a work that was never fully completed. The seventeenth century marble *Crucifix* is considered to be the work of Valerio Cioli.

The completion of the choir dates to 1860. It was carried out by Gaetano Baccani working in a Brunelleschian style typical of the imitative eclecticism of the late nineteenth century. The dome was frescoed by Vincenzo Meucci with the *Florentine Saints in Glory* and, in the pendentives, the *Four Fathers of the Church* (Gregory, Augustine, Jerome, Ambrose). Commissioned by Anna Maria Lodovica de' Medici and executed in 1742 the decoration is characteristic of the joyful eighteenth century Florentine style with its atmos-

pheric exuberance and Venetian influenced light tonality. The walls of the choir were originally frescoed with *Biblical Stories* and Pontormo's *Last Judgement*, whitewashed over in the eighteenth century.

The first chapel to the left of the High Altar (originally of the Rondinelli family) contains a painted wood *Madonna and Child* displayed in a glass reliquary on the altar. This fourteenth century statue is affectionately known as "La Bentornata" (the "Welcoming Madonna") because of her smiling and cordial expression. On the left wall is yet another example of San Lorenzo's wealth of Early Renaissance altarpieces – a *Nativity with Saints Julian and Francis* attributed to the school of Domenico Ghirlandaio.

On the altar of the second chapel (formerly belonging to the Ginori family) there is an altarpiece attributed to Davide Ghirlandaio with *Saint Anthony Abbot Enthroned with*

Aristodemo Costoli
Funerary monument to Pietro Benvenuti

View of the High Altar and the Choir with, in the
foreground, Andrea Verrocchio's *Sepulchral slab in
honour of Cosimo the Elder*

Saints Leonard and Julian. The lively predella
scenes depict *Episodes from the lives of the
three saints.* On the left wall is Giovanni
Dupré's *Monument to Berta Moltke Withfield*
(1864) executed in the gesticulatory style of
the Romantic period.

To the far side of the transept a fifteenth
century door, decorated with intarsia work,
gives access to the first Renaissance space conceived and built by Filippo Brunelleschi – the
Old Sacristy. (Although the name by which it
is traditionally known dates only from the
construction of Michelangelo's "New" Sacristy).

It is difficult not to marvel both at the
perfect and harmonious orchestration of its
architectural structure and its figural decoration which has remained unusually intact.
The whole room is a remarkable testimony to
the abilities of the most important artists active in Florence at the dawn of the
Renaissance. The Old Sacristy constitutes the
first experiment in architecture of the new
order, based on the relationship of those two
geometrical figures – the circle and the
square. An 'umbrella' ribbed dome is connected to the cube-shaped room by four
pendentives each decorated with a roundel.
At the base of the dome, *oculi* windows are
opened up in the arches between the ribs. The
walls of the Sacristy are lined with pilasters
supporting an entablature which runs around
the whole room. This is decorated with small
roundels containing heads of red seraphim
and blue cherubim related to Donatello's
workshop – it was on this occasion that the
sculptor experienced his most fruitful collaboration with Brunelleschi and his craftsmen;
the actual execution of these roundels is
thought to be by Luca della Robbia. The large
arches contain round-headed windows and
big roundels decorated with figures modelled
in coloured stucco. A small apse with a
frescoed dome repeats – on a small scale – the
form of the Sacristy, reinforcing the relationship between volumes and spaces which
characterizes the various parts of the room.

It was Giovanni de' Medici called Giovanni
di Bicci (1360-1429) who assigned to
Brunelleschi the building of the chapel. Dedicated to his patron saint St John the Evangelist, it was to serve both as a mausoleum for
himself and his wife Piccarda Bueri (d. 1433)
and as the sacristy of the church.

Work began in the autumn of 1422 and the
Sacristy was almost certainly completed in
1428; this date appears in the lantern of the
dome. It is thought that the decoration was
carried out between 1428 and 1432. The
extraordinary homogeneity between architecture and decoration (happily never interfered
with) makes of this space "the most integral
and complete architectural masterpiece of the
Early Renaissance" (Ruschi).

We enter the Sacristy through the elegant
intarsia-decorated doors, mentioned above.

Detail of the altar-frontal of the High Altar with
Giovan Battista Sassi's *Gathering of the Manna*

The gilded bronze door-knockers are modelled in the form of a diamond ring – one of
the Medici devices.

Around the walls are fifteenth century
walnut cupboards, finely decorated with ro-
sette and flowering amphora motifs – all
worked in intarsia. On the cupboard to the
right is a terracotta *Bust of St Lawrence*. This
is traditionally attributed to Donatello
although the pictorial subtlety of Desiderio

da Settignano has been detected in the work,
which dates from the middle of the fifteenth
century. At the centre of the room stands the
tomb of Giovanni di Bicci and his wife; it is
placed under a simple table of white marble
supported by bronze colonettes and marble
pillars. A porphyry disc is set into the table
top – summing up the formal simplicity of
Florentine Renaissance decorative art.

The sarcophagus, which dates to 1433, is

decorated with putti figures who hold up garlands of fruit, Medici coats of arms, and two tablets with the dedicatory inscriptions. It is attributed to Andrea di Lazzaro Cavalcanti, called "il Buggiano", Filippo Brunelleschi's adopted son. Unusually for a funerary monument dedicated not to a religious figure but to private citizens, it was possible to celebrate mass above their tomb.

Imaginative and visionary coloured stucco reliefs by Donatello decorate the upper register of the Sacristy – presumably dating to 1428-1432. To the south side, in the lunettes above the little doors, are *Saints Stephen and Lawrence* (to the left) and *Saints Cosmas and Damian* (to the right). The latter are thought not to be by Donatello's hand, although of his workshop; Michelozzo and Luca della Robbia are likely candidates.

On the walls appear the *Four Evangelists* – Saints Matthew, Mark, Luke and John who, as patron saint of the chapel, occupies the place of honour above the entrance arch to the apse. The pendentives contain scenes from the *Life of St John the Evangelist*; these stucco reliefs are modelled by Donatello himself in an animated and dramatic style. According to Manetti's biography of Brunelleschi, the very free handling of perspective space in these reliefs is supposed to have led to the proverbial quarrel between the two artists. Modelled in very low relief (Donatello's famous *stiacciato* technique) the roundels depict the *Raising of Drusiana, St John on Patmos*, the *Martyrdom* and the *Ascension of St John to Heaven*. Between 1984 and 1989 all these works underwent extensive restoration carried out by the Soprintendenza per i Beni ambientali e architettonici in collaboration with the Opificio delle Pietre Dure. The restoration freed the works from the accumulation of centuries and from the heavy layers added by successive attempts at restoration, thus revealing Donatello's use of delicate shades of colour based on tones of red and white.

The two small doors on either side of the altar chapel were Donatello's responsiblity and he decorated them with bronze reliefs. The panels depict the famous pairs of debating figures which did not meet with the approval of the classical purists of the period. In fact, the architect and sculptor Filarete

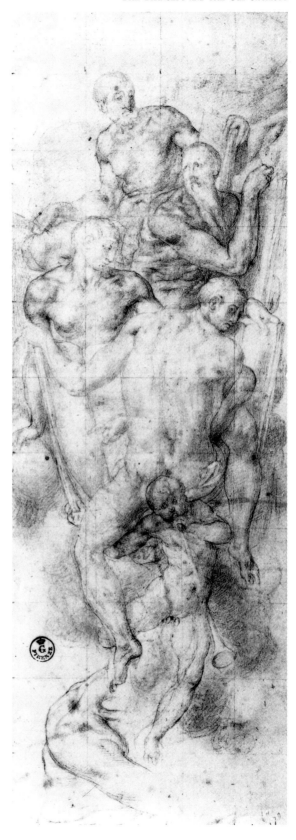

Jacopo Pontormo
Study for the *Deluge*.
Prints and Drawings Department, Uffizi

Vincenzo Meucci
Florentine Saints in Glory and the *Four Fathers of the
Church*

Fourteenth century
Madonna and Child
called "la Bentornata"
(the "Welcoming
Madonna")

dubbed them "the fencers" – a description at once ironic and polemical. In actual fact the doors are an exceptional testimony to the eclectic style of the Florentine sculptor. The right hand door illustrates *Doctrine* – St John the Baptist appears together with the apostles and the Fathers of the Church. The left door illustrates *Testimony* with figures of martyrs.

One enters the altar chapel between two marble balustrades of open-work carving decorated with motifs of amphoras sprouting elegant fronds of laurel, thought to be the work of Donatello. The altar itself was sculpted by Andrea di Lazzaro Cavalcanti and Pagno di Lapo Portigiani; its marble panels depict – at the centre – a *Madonna and Child*, flanked by two prophets – *Ezekial* and *Isaiah*. A fifteenth-century painted wood *Crucifix* (attributed to Simone di Nanni Ferrucci) hangs on the altar wall. Originally a triptych attributed to the school of Bernardo Daddi (second half of the fourteenth century) was given a somewhat incongruous placing below the cross. This has now been moved to the prior's residence. The

School of Domenico Ghirlandaio
Nativity with Saints Julian and Francis
and detail

Davide
Ghirlandaio
*St. Anthony Abbot
enthroned with
Saints Leonard
and Julian*

small cupola above the altar is decorated with one of the most unusual frescoes of the Early Renaissance in Florence. Above a pale grey frieze modelled to resemble a tightly rolled up curtain secured by gold ribbons, the dome opens up into a *Celestial Hemisphere*. This is thought to correspond to the astronomical chart of Florence on 4 July 1442. The position of the sun, the moon and the celestial bodies (represented by lively zodiacal signs) were probably indicated by the astronomer Paolo Dal Pozzo Toscanelli. The astrological figures have a somewhat heraldic feel – stylization combined with a Late Gothic vitality – which has led to their attribution to the Early Renaissance painter Giuliano d'Arrigo, known as "Pesello", by whom no certain work survives.

In the small chamber to the left of the altar chapel is another very remarkable Renaissance creation – a work of fantastical and intriguing forms: a *lavabo* supported on a plinth of green marble and framed by an arch in red marble. The back panel is decorated with a bas-relief. In the lunette a falcon grips between its talons a ribbon bearing the motto "semper" which was the device of Piero di Cosimo de' Medici. Below this, backed by a disc of serpentine, a sculpted mass rises up, consisting of bats' wings with lions' feet, supported by a goblet decorated with wolves' heads. The edge of this cup is garlanded with a wreath of oak leaves with, at the centre, the Medici coat of arms surrounded by the diamond ring device. The basin itself is decor-

ated with two winged sphinxes and, at the centre, a vigorously sculpted lion's head. This extraordinarily imaginative work of the 1470's is attributed to Verrocchio. On the left wall hangs a panel with a wood *Crucifixion* (probably late fifteenth century) with sixteenth century *Mourning figures* to the side of it. The framing pilasters of this altarpiece are decorated with symbols of the Passion of Christ.

Inserted into the wall which connects the Old Sacristy with the Chapel of Saints Cosmas and Damian – the Chapel of the Relics – is an absolute masterpiece of the second phase of the Florentine Renaissance: the *Funerary Monument of Piero "the Gouty" and of Giovanni de' Medici*. Made from a number of different materials – bronze, marble, porphyry, serpentine – and of unusual design, it became a reference point and source of inspiration for works of art in all media. It is clear from an early documentary source that the tomb was immediately recognized as being an exceptional work when it was unveiled in 1472: "the whole of Florence thronged to see it, almost as if they had been summoned to view one of the wonders of the world". The tomb was commissioned at Piero the Gouty's death in 1469 by his sons Lorenzo (later called "the Magnificent") and Giuliano to commemorate not only their father but also their uncle Giovanni; this explains the dedicatory inscription at the base of the monument: "Patri patruoque". The tomb was the work of Andrea Verrocchio who acted as a catalyst for new artistic ideas in Florence during this period. He created an ensemble that was rich in imaginative structural elements like the bronze open-work grille which separates the two spaces and the tortoise-shaped supports at the base. Verrocchio used bronze not only for the grille and the supports, mentioned above, but also for the wreath which encloses the inscription, for the paws – part animal, part vegetable – at the corners and for the decorative motifs of acanthus leaves and diamond rings. Stone was used for the outer frame and marble for the coat of arms and the inner frame which is carved with a very fine candelabra motif. Marble is also used for the inscribed base of the tomb and for the 'tiled' covering of the sarcophagus. The tomb itself

Fifteenth century door which gives access to the Old Sacristy

Giovanni Dupré
Monument to Berta Moltke Withfield

is made of porphyry and serpentine was chosen for the medallion bearing the inscription where traces of gold have been detected following the recent cleaning. Verrocchio's work is also rich in decorative elements and it is in this area that his refinement as a sculptor is particularly evident: the very delicate candelabra motifs of the marble surround which meet the bronze diamond at the top of the arch, the network of the grill, the sprays of foliage from which the lions' paws emerge, the decorative crown of the sarcophagus made up of a diamond motif combined with acanthus leaves and cornucopia. In addition, it seems that Verrocchio wanted to create the polychromatic look of the tomb solely through the natural colours of the materials

External view of
the cupola of the
Old Sacristy

Views of the main
dome over
Brunelleschi's Old
Sacristy with, on
the right, the
unusual small
cupola frescoed
with a *Celestial
Hemisphere*

The interior of the Old Sacristy

Detail of the cornice of the Old Sacristy decorated with angels' heads, probably the work of Luca della Robbia

Donatello
St. Matthew.
Old Sacristy

Donatello
St. Mark.
Old Sacristy

Donatello
St. John the Evangelist.
Old Sacristy

Donatello
St. Luke.
Old Sacristy

he used. This idea demonstrates the skilful planning of the Verrocchio workshop and the absolute mastery in the handling of various techniques.

It is worth noting that this remarkable work inspired Leonardo da Vinci when he came to paint the Virgin's lectern in his Uffizi *Annunciation*. It is clear that the significance of this monument could not have been lost on this young artist newly released from the Verrocchio workshop.

With this work the Old Sacristy therefore boasted yet another enormously important work of art as part of its decoration, a work which so clearly expresses the creative tension of the Florentine Renaissance. Such was the significance of the chapel that an unknown fifteenth century poet dedicated the following lines to it. They come from *"Terze Rime"* in *honour of Cosimo de' Medici*, published by Fabriczy:

"Et dall'un lato è una sagrestia
che mai più ve ne fu una più bella,

Donatello
St. John on Patmos.
Old Sacristy

Donatello
Raïsing of Drusiana.
Old Sacristy

Donatello
Martyrdom of St. John.
Old Sacristy

Donatello
The Ascension of St. John.
Old Sacristy

Andrea di Lazzaro Cavalcanti
Sarcophagus of Giovanni di Bicci and Piccarda Bueri.
Old Sacristy

Donatello or Desiderio da Settignano
Bust of St. Lawrence.
Old Sacristy

Donatello
Saints Stephen and Lawrence.
Old Sacristy

Workshop of Donatello
Saints Cosmas and Damian.
Old Sacristy

Donatello
The Martyrs' Door.
Old Sacristy

Donatello
The Apostles' Door.
Old Sacristy

et sì maravigliosa, et sì giulìa,
che chi la mira fiso par ch'abbagli,
perché per tutto par che sol vi sia."

"And to one side is a sacristy/ Whose beauty was never to be surpassed, /And so wondrous, and so joyous / That whoever gazed at it was dazzled / Because the sun seems to shine throughout".

To the right of the Sacristy is the Chapel of Saints Cosmas and Damian, also called the Chapel of the Relics. On either side of the entrance arch, facing the church, there are two frescoes: to the right *Saints Cosmas and Damian* and, to the left, *Saint Carlo Borromeo with another Prelate*, dated 1611 and attributed to Bernardino Poccetti. On the altar is an early fourteenth century panel – the *Madonna del Latte* (the Virgin suckling the Christ Child). This is inserted into an altarpiece by Francesco Conti depicting *Saints Zenobius, Lawrence and Ambrose* (1717). This canvas serves as a reminder of the foundation of the basilica since tradition has it that the two bishop saints (Zenobius and Ambrose)

49

Detail of Donatello's *Martyrs' Door* showing Saints
Lawrence and Stephen

Detail of Donatello's *Martyrs' Door* showing two
martyr saints

Detail of Donatello's *Apostles' Door* showing Saints
Peter and Paul

Detail of Donatello's *Apostles' Door* showing two
Fathers of the Church

consecrated the church. The inscription on
the altar recalls how the image of the
Madonna and Child once hung in the bed-
room of Saint Zenobius – a clearly apocry-
phal, though charming, story. The inscription
also unusually refers to Cosimo III as "King
of the Tuscans" which leads one to think of
the penultimate Granduke's imminent coron-
ation. This event, of course, never took place

and in consequence caused the last phase of
Medicean Granducal rule to be overshadowed
by a feeling of melancholy frustration at the
inevitable end of the dynasty.

The great cupboards of the chapel contain
relics collected by Lorenzo the Magnificent
and by the Medici popes – Leo X and Clement VII. They were arranged here in 1778
following the removal to the Uffizi Gallery of

Giuliano d'Arrigo called "Pesello"
Small cupola of the Old Sacristy with its *Celestial
Hemisphere* fresco

Details from the
Celestial Hemisphere
painted by Giuliano
d'Arrigo called
"Pesello" in the small
cupola of the Old
Sacristy

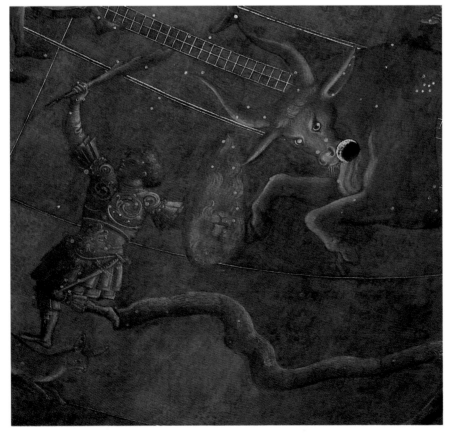

Andrea Verrocchio
Lavabo.
Small chamber to the
left of the Old Sacristy

Andrea Verrocchio: *Funerary Monument of Piero the Gouty and Giovanni de' Medici.* Old Sacristy

a number of reliquaries (particularly the vases in rare or precious materials); the latter are now in the Museo degli Argenti (the Silver Museum, Palazzo Pitti). In 1945 there was a further transfer of some of the most important reliquaries – this time to the Medici Chapels where they remain today. The Chapel of the Relics houses the very oldest reliquaries together with other religious objects; they are stored in the left hand cupboard – the wooden doors of which are embellished with elegant leafy motifs in appliquéd wood – and in the two recessed wall niches lined with red silk.

The chapel to the left belonged to the Martelli family. The Renaissance-style *Cenotaph* on the right wall commemorates Donatello. The sculptor, who died in 1466, is buried in the crypt of the church. The monument was made in 1896 by Dario Guidotti and Raffaello Romanelli. On the altar is Fra Filippo Lippi's panel of the *Annunciation*. It is without doubt one of the Carmelite monk's most attractive works. Here the rigorous Masacciesque perspective becomes a more complex series of coherently organized spaces beginning with the division of the painting using a fictive central pilaster. In addition, the altarpiece shows Lippi's sense of proud humanity tempered into a feeling of expressive warmth. Noteworthy for its symbolic and mystical intensity is the glass bottle of water (a symbol of the virginity of Mary) inserted into the step of the 'stage'. The work is datable to between 1437 and 1441. The graceful style of Lippi's colleague Francesco Pesellino has been detected in the predella panels depicting the *Stories of Saint Nicholas* and the Martelli coat of arms. Originally, these were probably quite unrelated to the main panel.

An expressive painted wooden *Crucifix* is inserted into the window opening; some believe it to be related to German art. On the left wall there is the most unusual *Sarcophagus of Niccolò and Fioretta Martelli*. Dated to about 1450 and thought to be by Donatello, it has the appearance of wicker basket-work. The heraldic griffon of the Martelli coat of arms decorates the sides. Above the tomb hangs a canvas depicting *St Jerome and the angel*, a seventeenth century work by Giuseppe Nicola Nasini from Monte Amiata.

Bernardino Poccetti
Saints Cosmas and Damian.
Left transept

Anonymous fourteenth
century
Madonna del Latte,
framed by Francesco
Conti's *Saints Zenobius,
Lawrence and Ambrose.*
Chapel of the Relics

Cupboard containing
reliquaries and other
liturgical objects.
Chapel of the Relics

Filippo Lippi
Annunciation and detail.
Martelli Chapel

Dario Guidotti and Raffaello Romanelli
Cenotaph to Donatello.
Martelli Chapel

German school of the fifteenth century
Crucifix.
Martelli Chapel

Donatello (attrib.)
Sarcophagus of Niccolò and Fioretta Martelli.
Martelli Chapel

The Left Aisle

The left side of the church also boasts a series of important works of art. This is immediately obvious in the large fresco, on the wall of the left aisle, depicting the *Martyrdom of St Lawrence*. This is a late work by Agnolo Bronzino; commissioned by Duke Cosimo I himself in 1565, it was completed in 1569. The fresco is a good indication of the eclectic and erudite Mannerist style in which borrowings from Michelangelo mingle with influences from classical art.

In front of the fresco is Donatello's left *Pulpit* which shares its history with its pendant opposite. Here the seventeenth century additions of fictive bronze panels in painted wood are those of the *Flagellation* and *St John the Evangelist*. Therefore, the scenes of the *Agony in the Garden*, the *Crucifixion, Christ before Pilate and Caiaphas* and the frenzied, dramatic *Deposition* are by Donatello and his assistants.

The *Cantoria* (choir stall) on the aisle wall is also from Donatello's workshop. It is a work of astonishing decorative variety, consisting of consoles, panels, colonettes, niches and a frieze of winged shells. The *Cantoria* illustrates both the lively, imaginative quality of Donatellian works and the wealth of techniques employed. These range from carving, to inlays, mosaic work and the handling of different kinds of marble.

Returning to the altarpieces of the side chapels we have, in the sixth (formerly of the Aldobrandini family) an engaging work by Pietro Annigoni: *St Joseph and the Christ Child in the Carpentry Workshop*, an unusual contemporary contribution to the historic decoration of the basilica.

In the following chapel (of the Taddei family) an altarpiece depicting the *Crucifixion of St Acasio* can be connected with the classicising movement in sixteenth century Florentine art; the painter is Giovanni Antonio Sogliani. The predella panels illustrating *Scenes from the life of St Acasio*, now in the Uffizi, were painted by Bachiacca. The altarpiece was commissioned in 1521 by Alfonsina Orsini, widow of Piero di Lorenzo de' Medici (called "il Fatuo" – "the Fatuous" sometimes called Piero "the Unfortunate"). In the fourth chapel (of the Cambini family) there hangs a wooden *Crucifix*. This fifteenth century work is possibly of the German school and by the same hand as the one in the Martelli chapel. It is flanked by two seventeenth century *Mourning Figures* painted on carved wood by Lorenzo Lippi.

The third chapel (formerly of the Altoviti family) has as its altarpiece a carefully executed work by the nineteenth century painter Zanobi Canovai: the *Enthroned Madonna and Child with Saints Lawrence and Zenobius* (1877). In the second chapel, which originally came under the patronage of the Medici family, the eighteenth century altarpiece of the *Crucifixion with Mourning Figures* is by Francesco Conti. And, finally, in the first chapel (of the Ubaldini family) there is the *Calling of St Matthew* painted by Pietro Marchesini in a classicising style.

Agnolo Bronzino
Martyrdom of St. Lawrence

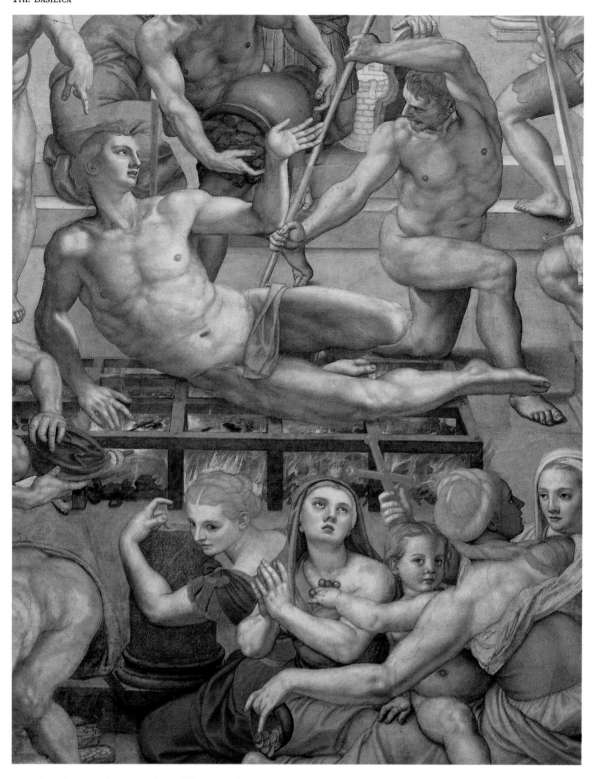

Detail of Bronzino's *Martyrdom of St. Lawrence*

Donatello
Left *Pulpit*

Detail of Donatello's *Pulpit* showing the *Agony in the Garden*

Details of Donatello's *Pulpit* showing the *Deposition* and the *Entombment*

Pietro Annigoni
St. Joseph and the Christ Child in the Carpentry Workshop

The left aisle with in the foreground the *Cantoria* (Choir Stall) by the workshop of Donatello

Giovanni Antonio Sogliani
Crucifixion of St. Acasio

Wooden Crucifix by a German artist of the fifteenth century and *Two Grieving figures* by Lorenzo Lippi

THE CLOISTERS

This, then, is the remarkable artistic endowment of the basilica. A panoramic vision of six hundred years of supreme examples of Florentine art, perfectly integrated into one of the most important Renaissance buildings. The rest of the complex associated with the church is also of great interest, beginning with the cloister. Access to this is either through the entrance to the far left of the facade (on the Piazza San Lorenzo) or through the door which opens off the left hand aisle, near the Donatellian *Cantoria*.

The Brunelleschian cloister (where the prior and canons of San Lorenzo have their living quarters) consists of two superimposed loggias, the lower one arcaded and the upper with an architrave. Both are supported by Ionic columns, placed exactly on an axis; a string-course runs above the arcade indicating the level of the floor of the upper loggia. The cloister gives a feeling of rare harmony and calm serenity. This is achieved through the perfect rhythm of the spatial relationships of the building and even through the inspired planting of the central space with a parterre of box. The views from the upper floor of the cloister are delightful: to the north is the flank of the church, and its lantern together with the great tiled dome of the Chapel of the Princes; to the east the imposing dome of the Cathedral.

Even the walls of the cloister (especially in the lower corridor) are not without works of art and historical memorials. Near the entrance, there is a stucco panel of the *Madonna and Child*, in the style of Desiderio da Settignano. The glazed terracotta frame – dated 1513 – was reworked in the nineteenth century. Various memorial tablets are also of the nineteenth century – these commemorate those buried in the crypt of the church. An inscription framed by sumptuous green marble (which has something of the late Baroque style of Foggini) records the contributions of the Electress Palatine Anna Maria Lodovica de' Medici to the completion of the basilica. In a niche at the end of the corridor stands the tense image of *Paolo Giovio*, bishop of Como, historian and art collector. The statue, a work of 1560 sculpted by Francesco di Giuliano da Sangallo, has a definite Mannerist flavour.

The pedimented door to the left, flanked by two mullioned windows indicates the Chapel of the Chapter of Canons, a narrow fifteenth century room lined with the choir-stalls of the canons. These are both carved and decorated with intarsia work. The back panels are embellished with amphora motifs of various kinds – very similar to the style of the cupboards in the Old Sacristy.

Next to the Brunelleschian cloister is a second cloister, separated from the main one by a corridor which houses the residence of the prior of the basilica (who, because of his high ecclesiastical office is authorised to wear a mitre – an indication of the great importance of San Lorenzo). This much narrower cloister is closed by a high wall with small polygonal piers which presumably relate to the pre-Brunelleschian building.

The door between the Chapel of the Chapter and the *Monument to Paolo Giovio* gives access to the crypt of the basilica. Here is the floor tomb of Donatello and the *Sepulchre of Cosimo the Elder* contained within a stocky pier and decorated with a strigil-pattern frieze. Set into the four sides, faced with serpentine stone, Medici coats of arms alternate with curious crosses with three vertical arms. The *oculi* openings in the vault of the crypt allow light to filter through from the presbytery of the church. This unusual monument (which dates to after 1464) has been given to Verrocchio as has the marble sepulchral slab on the floor of the church above.

A gate separates this subterranean area of the church (on the walls of which – following the 1966 flood – inscribed tablets and coats of arms have been arranged) from the Crypt of the House of Lorraine. It is a place of great sobriety. The colour scheme – an interplay of the white of marble and plaster with the grey of the stone – seems to symbolize the discreet presence of a dynasty who were concerned not so much with self-celebration as with the well-being of their subjects – as is witnessed by their numerous public works.

View of Brunelleschi's cloister looking towards the
dome of the Chapel of the Princes

The cloister with the dome of Santa Maria del Fiore
and Giotto's bell-tower in the background

Francesco da Sangallo
Statue of Paolo Giovio

Fifteenth century wooden choir-stalls, carved and
decorated with intarsia work.
Chapel of the Chapter of Canons

Tomb of Cosimo the Elder in the crypt of the basilica

The central pier bears the memorial tablets
of the four Grandukes of the House of
Lorraine. Among these only Ferdinando III is
buried in the Crypt. The others who became
emperors (like Francesco Stefano and Pietro
Leopoldo) or who died in exile (like
Leopoldo II) are buried elsewhere. On the
walls and floor of the Crypt the tablets commemorate other members of the Hapsburg-
Lorraine lineage and personalities who were
related to them.

View of the Crypt of the House of Lorraine in the
subterranean area of the basilica

The Laurentian Library

THE LAURENTIAN LIBRARY

On the first floor of the Brunelleschian cloister is the entrance to the Laurentian Library which houses what must be considered the most important and prestigious collection of antique books in Italy. It comprises the most lasting cultural inheritance which the Medici family has passed down to the attention, care and admiration of posterity. The collection had its genesis in the humanistic interests of Cosimo the Elder and his attendance of the Academy of Roberto de' Rossi. There followed his friendship with Niccolò Niccoli with whom he shared a passion for collecting ancient manuscripts of the works of classical authors. With Niccoli's guidance Cosimo acquired a great number of these. At the former's death, in 1437, Cosimo inherited most of Niccoli's library and donated a great many of these manuscripts to the monastery of San Marco. He also founded the library at the Badia Fiesolana. He was assisted in his acquisitions for this collection by Vespasiano da Bisticci who provided copyists with classical texts for subsequent diffusion. The original nucleus of volumes was then added to by Cosimo's son Piero. Subsequently Lorenzo completed the collection with the acquisition of, above all, Greek texts. The library followed the ups and downs of the Medici family. In 1494, following the sentence of exile imposed on Piero the Unfortunate and the banishment from Florence of the whole of the Medici family the library was confiscated by the Republican government and absorbed *in toto* into the library of the San Marco monastery. In 1508 it was recovered by Cardinal Giovanni de' Medici (the second son of Lorenzo the Magnificent – he became Pope Leo X) who transferred it to Rome. His successor Clement VII (Giulio de' Medici, son of

Two views of the entrance vestibule to the Laurentian Library designed by Michelangelo

The fantastical staircase leading to the Laurentian Library, carried out by Bartolommeo Ammannati to Michelangelo's model

Giuliano di Piero) brought the collection back to Florence in 1523 and immediately commissioned Michelangelo to design a library to house it. This was to be another very important project for Michelangelo – he made preparatory drawings for it and concerned himself with its construction for ten years before his definitive departure for Rome in 1534. However, he did not relinquish control of the project, monitoring the phases of building as the work was continued by his followers Giorgio Vasari and Bartolommeo Ammannati, who also completed Michelangelo's New Sacristy and who were assiduous in following the master's plans.

The decoration of the library went hand in hand with its actual construction (the ceiling dates to 1549-1550, the flooring from 1549-1554, the windows from 1558-1568) thus making the library one of the most unified works of the High Renaissance (or should we say of Mannerism) to be found in Florence.

The reading-room of the Laurentian Library

Detail of the monumental desks (*plutei*) of the reading-room

Details illustrating the decorative connection between the ceiling (above) – the work of Giovan Battista Del Tasso and Carota – and the floor of the Library carried out by Santi Buglioni

The vast reading-room is preceded by the dramatic entrance vestibule (called the *ricetto*) planned in elevation by Michelangelo and built in that characteristic Florentine two-one combination of grey sand-stone elements on white plaster. Here Michelangelo's energetic and powerfully modelled architectural vocabulary (free from the constraints of the Brunelleschian style imposed on him, to a certain extent, in the New Sacristy) emerges in the tabernacle niches, the paired columns, the portal – all imbued with a feeling of solid strength. This dynamism, concentrated on the walls of the vestibule, overflows in the fantastical staircase (built by Ammannati in 1559, following a clay model prepared by Michelangelo). It consists of three flights of steps; the outer ones are quadrangular shaped, the central ones convex – and the bottom three steps are completely elliptical. The staircase is, then, an explosion of originality which fits perfectly with the fanciful character of the Mannerist style of architecture. The vertical tensions of the vestibule seem to quieten down in the long hall of the big reading-room. Here the guiding principle of the design is the maxi-

One of the original windows of the Laurentian Library with the device of Cosimo I

mum use made of the lateral sources of light. The entire space possesses a strong sense of formal homogeneity like few other interiors. All aspects of the library are unified – the *plutei* for example – the inlaid wooden desks designed by Michelangelo himself and which still retain the small placques inscribed with the number of the manuscripts originally kept on each desk. The *plutei* were made by the woodworkers Battista del Cinque and Ciapino and their decoration was echoed in the elaborate ceiling along with motifs of wreaths, ribbons and volutes, carried out by Giovan Battista Del Tasso and Carota. The same decoration is picked up in the mellow tones of red and yellow of the worn terracotta floor. This was made by Santi Buglioni (a follower of the Della Robbia workshop) basing himself on the designs of Niccolò Tribolo – another pupil and follower of Michelangelo.

Further evidence of the homogeneity of the decoration of the Laurentian Library is provided by the survival of the original windows. These are painted in grisaille on an ochre-coloured background and contain – besides grotesques, cherubs and garlands – the coat of arms and devices of Pope Clement VII and of Cosimo I. The large room is filled with the warm, diffused light which filters through these painted panes of glass. Marchini has attributed the designs for these windows to Giorgio Vasari himself and to his closest collaborator on the rennovation of the Palazzo Vecchio – Marco da Faenza.

On the right of the reading-room a door leads to the Neoclassical "Tribuna d'Elci" (called the 'Rotonda') designed by the architect Pasquale Poccianti in 1841 to house the collection of precious manuscripts, incunabula and drawings given to the State by Angelo Maria d'Elci.

The bibliographical collections of the Laurentian Library are of exceptional importance for the history of written documents, illuminated manuscripts, and for the history of publishing both in Florence and elsewhere in Italy. The importance of the Florentine school of illuminated manuscripts, from the thirteenth to the sixteenth centuries, is well documented by the collection. In fact, the work of the monastic *scriptorium* of the Monastero degli Angeli is represented by

Lorenzo Monaco, and that of San Marco by Attavante, Gherardo and Monte del Fuora. Humanistic illuminated manuscripts are represented by Francesco d'Antonio del Chierico, Filippo Torelli and Boccardino. In addition, the other collections housed in the library are important because they so clearly illustrate the Medici family's particular passion for collecting – which was not confined to works of art. What is also evident is their scholarly interest in the production of books which is so characteristic of Italian culture up to the end of the nineteenth century. So the prominence of the Laurentian Library consists of the juxtaposition of bibliographical rarities with texts (precious objects in themselves) essential to scholarly research. A summary description will give some idea of the most significant items in the collection: Greco-Roman papyri, the Byzantine version of Justinian's *Pandects*, Evangelisteries of the Eastern Church, the *Amiatinus Bible* of the seventh or eighth century, the only manuscript of the *Annales* of Tacitus, Horace's *Odes (Carmina)* with a gloss by Petrarch, Dante's *Divine Comedy* annotated by Filippo Villani, the *Biadaiolo Codex*, an essential document for information about fourteenth century Florentine society. This is just a small sample of the patrimony of this prestigious collection which owes its origins to the inexhaustible cultural curiosity of the Medici family.

The *Cassetta Cesarini*, fifteenth century Florentine goldsmith work

Miniature from the *Biadaiolo Codex* illustrating the Florentines assisting the poor people banished from Siena

Miniature from the *Biadaiolo Codex* showing the sale of grain

Miniature from the *Logic* of Aristotle illustrated by Francesco d'Antonio del Chierico showing portraits of Cosimo the Elder and Piero de' Medici in the medallions of the frame

Miniature of the prophet Ezra from the *Amiatinus Bible*

THE "MEDICI CHAPELS"

Access to the complex known collectively as the "Medici Chapels" (now a museum and comprising the Crypt of the Granducal family, the Chapel "of the Princes", and Michelangelo's New Sacristy) is through a marble framed entrance on the Piazza degli Aldobrandini (no. 6).

And so we come to yet another series of monumental rooms which are as closely linked to the history of the Medici family as they are to the church of San Lorenzo. They were planned to serve as memorials to the family and to become (as they did) the Medici mausoleum, a celebration of a dynasty which for three hundred years dominated their native city and subsequently the whole of Tuscany.

From the historical and artistic point of view the most outstanding part of the "Medici Chapels" is without doubt Michelangelo's New Sacristy (so named to distinguish it from Brunelleschi's earlier sacristy) where both architecture and sculpture are expressive of Michelangelo's imaginative creativity. From the outside the New Sacristy appears as a quadrangular addition; the ground plan of the church shows it to be in absolute symmetry with the Old Sacristy which is situated on the opposite side of the cross-arm. The cupola is covered with curved, overlapping tiles, and topped by a marble lantern of great inventiveness; in the form of a pavilion, it is decorated with a series of ornamental lions' heads in gilded copper which allude to the name of the promoter of this architectural project – Pope Leo X.

The cupola of the New Sacristy

The Chapel of the Princes with the entrance to the museum complex of the Medici Chapels

The Chapel of the Princes

The more imposing building is, however, the Chapel of the Princes which, being an extension of the crossing and choir of the church of San Lorenzo, has to be seen as its chancel or "Cappella Maggiore". On the architectural skyline of Florence its dome is second only to that of Santa Maria del Fiore (the "Duomo") with which it invites both comparison and contrast. The tonality of the tiled covering is the same although the colours of its drum are not and provide a counterpoint to that of the "Duomo". The Chapel of the Princes dome is smaller than that of the Cathedral and it is as if this is the architectural expression of the attentuation of the domineering temporal force of the Medici dynasty faced with the superiority of religious authority.

The lower part of the exterior consists of a high octagonal base, pierced by exedras with their respective convex tribunes, closely flanked by quadrangular buttresses – with inserts of marble – reaching to the drum of the dome. It is not difficult to detect here, too, something of the dynamic structural organiza-

The dome of the Chapel of the Princes with its huge windows with marble surrounds designed by Ferdinando and Giuseppe Ruggieri

Wooden model (c. 1740) by Ferdinando and Giuseppe Ruggieri for the completion of the dome of the Chapel of the Princes

tion of the east end of the Cathedral. Up to this point the architect was Matteo Nigetti who, from 1604, was in charge of the construction of the Medici mausoleum under the supervision of Don Giovanni de' Medici, illegitimate son of Leopoldo I and himself an architect.

Large windows open up in the drum; these are topped by curvilinear pediments and are framed by curiously undulating surrounds of white marble looking, towards the bottom, like flapping stoles. These were designed in the 1740's by Ferdinando and Giuseppe Ruggieri on the instigation of the Electress Palatine Anna Maria Lodovica. The projected

lantern was also the responsibility of Ferdinando Ruggieri. This was to have mirrored the design of that of the "Duomo" but it was never built. Today the top of the cupola consists of a simple glass skylight with a pyramidal metal frame.

On entering the Medici Chapels complex the first area one encounters is the Crypt where members of the Granducal branch of the Medici family are buried. It is a low-ceilinged, almost cross-shaped space, divided by quadrangular piers. Small tribunes open up in the walls, illuminated by low arched windows. Each one contains the remains of a Granduke (corresponding to the appropriate funerary monument in the chapel above); the closest relatives of each are also buried here. On the floor, enlivened with flagstones of marble and *pietra forte* (the local tan-coloured stone), are arranged the marble sepulchral slabs of members of the Medici family with their bronze inscriptions indicating the name, immediate ancestry, rank and dates of birth and death of each. Brass barriers have recently been erected around the slabs and their frames to protect them from being worn down by the passage of visitors.

The present arrangement of the Crypt was instigated by Leopoldo II in 1858 – as is testified by the marble inscription in Latin behind the altar. He wished to restore order and dignity to this burial place following the exhumation and identification of the bodies between September 18-25, 1857. Before the coffins had simply been placed on the floor. The creation of the entrance from Piazza Madonna also dates from this period.

The architecture of the Crypt, which retains that characteristic feeling of Florentine measure, is somewhat archaic in its use of domed vaults and in that familiar two-toned effect of grey sandstone on white plaster. The project seems to have been the responsibility of Bernardo Buontalenti (from 1602) who elaborated on the original ideas drawn up by Don Giovanni de' Medici for the entire Medici mausoleum complex. Matteo Nigetti succeeded Buontalenti, working through the various phases of the transformation of the imposing construction in the period between 1605 and about 1640.

The marble, classicizing altar at the back of the Crypt (where every year masses for the souls of the dead are still held for the Medici dynasty) forms part of the nineteenth century reorganization initiated by Pietro Leopoldo. On either side of the altar are sixteenth century statues of *Mourning Figures*, the work of Felice Palma. According to Parronchi, these were originally intended to flank – in the same Crypt – Valerio Cioli's *Crucifix* which is now on the High Altar of the basilica itself. On the right is the wooden model of the cupola of the Chapel of the Princes with its marble lantern designed by Ferdinando Ruggieri in about 1740.

Two flights of steps lead to the upper floor

Section drawing of the decoration of the Chapel of the Princes by Ferdinando Ruggieri.
Prints and Drawings Department, Uffizi

The great crypt which houses the remains of the Medici grandukes initiated by Bernardo Buontalenti

and right at their beginning are two Baroque style holy-water fonts sculpted from green marble. On both flights appear tablets decorated with, on one side heads of Mary and the Angel Gabriel which are related to the iconography of the *Annunciation* painting in the church of Santissima Annunziata, and on the other a Crucifix. These tablets recall the history of the foundation of the Chapel of the Princes from 1605 to 1640.

The Chapel of the Princes opens out as an enormous space of great height; in fact, it gives the impression of being more spacious than it actually is. The facing in inlays of variegated marbles and semi-precious stone (arranged in sobre alternations of green and red) imparts a sedate splendour to the place. The high dado is decorated with thirty-two funerary urns fashioned from inlays of red "Barga" jasper and green "Corsica" jasper. These alternate with the sixteen coats of arms of those granducal cities which were diocesan sees: Pienza, Chiusi, Sovana, Montalcino, Grosseto, Pisa, Massa di Maremma, Siena, Fiesole, Pistoia, Florence, Borgo Sansepolcro, Volterra, Arezzo, Montepulciano, Cortona.

Above are the six cenotaphs of the Medici Grandukes (there was no room for the last of these – Gian Gastone) consisting of porphyry tombs each with its cushion bearing the granducal crown decorated, at the central point, with a lily. Above the tombs are niches which were intended to display the sculpted image of each prince. It is interesting to read the chapel as an allegory of princely power stemming from territorial possession here symbolised, of course, by the coats of arms of the Tuscan *civitates*.

Each of the tomb niches is flanked by giant pilasters crowned with gilded bronze capitals. The civic coats of arms are composed of semi-precious stones (*pietre dure*) and other very rare and precious materials – different kinds of jasper, polychromatic marbles, alabasters, quartz of various kinds, lapis lazuli, coral and mother-of-pearl. The arms were assembled in the granducal workshops at the end of the sixteenth century. In fact, Ferdinando I, having taken up again Cosimo I's dream of a magnificent family mausoleum, founded, in 1588, the "Opificio delle Pietre Dure" expressly for the purpose of the collecting and

The opulent interior of the Chapel of the Princes

Some of the civic coats of arms which decorate the dado of the Chapel of the Princes

Pietro and Ferdinando Tacca
Sarcophagus and statue of Granduke Ferdinando I de' Medici

Pietro Tacca
Sarcophagus and statue of Granduke Cosimo II de' Medici

working of stones and precious marbles required for the embellishment of the great Medici memorial. The "Opificio" (or "Works") still functions today as an institute specializing in the restoration of major works of art as well as *objets d'art*; it operates not solely in Florence but over the whole country. The only niches to be filled with statues of the Grandukes were those of Ferdinando II and his son Cosimo II. The portrait of the former, in gilded bronze, was carried out by Pietro and Ferdinando Tacca between 1626 an 1631. The bronze statue of Cosimo is the work of Pietro Tacca (1626 to after 1642). Both Medici princes are dressed in the opulent ceremonial costume of the Grand Masters of the Knightly Order of Saint Stephen – damask robes with ermine capes.

The choir of the chapel consists of a tribune illuminated by three large windows; it has a coffered vault decorated with marble rosettes. The altar is placed to the front of the choir; its original design was carried out by Bernardo Buontalenti. Judging from the surviving drawings it was intended to be particularly grandiose, together with the projected ciborium it would have filled the whole arched area behind. According to contemporary accounts the materials employed on this altar and its decorative panels were of particularly high quality and of great refinement. After 1728, when the altar was almost complete, it was dismantled and its components dispersed. And so the Chapel of the Princes was deprived of what was to have been its most important adornment. In 1821 an attempt was made by the architect Cacialli to reconstruct the altar (the related drawings are in the Museum of the "Opificio delle Pietre Dure") but the project came to nothing. The history of this altar with all those interruptions and suspensions – which characterized the whole mausoleum project and its decoration – finds a curious parallel in the fortunes of the Granducal family itself. Their own history had been interrupted, as it were, just as the Grand Duchy seemed to be on the edge of elevation to a kingdom – that ultimate goal so craved by the last Medici. The story of the altar reached a most unusual conclusion between 1927 and 1937. Amedeo Orlandini, director of the "Opificio delle Pietre Dure", was requested to present a provisional solution, making use of those pre-existing altar parts from former versions. The whole altar was finally put together in 1937 to coincide with a proposed visit of Adolf Hitler to the Laurentian complex (which then never took place). So, the present altar is a wooden structure painted to imitate porphyry. Into this are inserted *pietre dure* panels from various centuries – some worked in relief, some inlaid. Amongst these the panels on the front of the altar are of particularly fine quality: the one decorated with liturgical objects designed by Giovan Battista Giorgi (c. 1850) and Augusto Betti's *Supper at Emmaus* (1861). Even the candlesticks are of lathed wood, painted to resemble porphyry.

Since 1945 the two small side rooms situated behind the altar have been used to house reliquaries and liturgical objects – from various periods and of different kinds of workmanship – donated by the Medici family to their patronal church. Some of these belonged to the collection of Lorenzo the Magnificent, for example, the Roman rock crystal reliquary of eastern Islamic manufacture. A very valuable mitre, decorated with small pearls, was donated by Pope Leo X as well as a silver crosier, made in Rome in the sixteenth century, which has in the crook a figure, in the round, of Saint Lawrence. The majority of the other reliquaries were designed and made in the granducal workshops. They must be considered as real works of art and masterpieces of the applied arts in Florence. This is particularly true of the Baroque pieces which are conceived with a strong sense of the theatrical and executed with an absolute mastery of the precious materials, some of which – the *pietre dure* especially – were very difficult to work. Some of the most important seventeenth and eighteenth century artists in Florence worked on the more significant of these church ornaments. The style of Giovan Battista Foggini is evident in the *Reliquary of Saint Sigismund*, and that of Massimiliano Soldani Benzi in the *Reliquary of Saint Casimir* and the *Reliquary of Saint Alessio*. The latter has a fantastical and precious setting created with ebony, gilded bronze and semi-precious stones. Then there is Giuseppe Antonio Torricelli, a master of

Augusto Betti
Supper at Emmaus, panel from the altar worked in
inlays of semi-precious stone (*pietre dure*)

Giovan Battista Giorgi
Pietre dure altar panels decorated with liturgical
objects

Giuseppe Antonio Torricelli
Reliquary of St. Emeric (overleaf)

Giovan Battista Foggini
Reliquary of St. Sigismund (on the following page)

Two gifts of Pope Leo X: a *mitre* decorated with pearls and a silver *crosier* made in Rome

Islamic manufacture and Venetian goldsmith work *Reliquary of the Virgin Martyr Erina*, engraved crystal

carving *pietre dure* in the round, whose work is represented by the *Reliquary of Saint Ambrose* and that of *Saint Mary of Egypt*. The work of Cosimo Merlini, silversmith to the granducal court, is also present in this collection. Other examples are of northern European manufacture – German and Flemish. These came with the patrimony of the Granduchesses who, like Anne of Austria, were often foreigners.

The vault of the cupola was to have been

Massimiliano Soldani
Benzi
Reliquary of St. Casimir

Reliquary of St. Ambrose
designed by Giovan
Battista Foggini and
executed by Antonio
Torricelli

The nineteenth century
floor decorated with
Medici coats of arms

covered with lapis lazuli coffering studded with gilded bronze rosettes – yet another ostentatious and lavish project destined to remain unrealized. The Medici were not able to carry it out and the House of Lorraine, who inherited the responsibility for the chapel's completion, had the vault decorated with gilded stucco surrounds in the form of great garlands and commissioned Pietro Benvenuti to paint the segments of the cupola (1828-1837). In a style which is a mixture of the Neoclassical (rare in Florence) and the Michelangelesque, Benvenuti painted a cycle of frescoes which enjoyed great renown in Florence at the time. The scenes depict episodes from the Old and New Testaments

The octagon of the dome with gilded stucco garland surrounds and frescoed by Pietro Benvenuti with Old and New Testament scenes which illustrate the theme of the spiritual as well as the physical aspects of Death. Figures of Prophets and the Evangelists are depicted in the hexagonal panels of the vault.

In 1874 the last work was carried out in the Medici mausoleum – the flooring. Using mainly green Corsican marble the decoration reproduces the Medici coat of arms. It was designed by Edoardo Marchionni who was also the director of the "Opificio delle Pietre Dure" thus reconfirming that close, centuries-old tie between the Florentine institute and the building that had allowed for its very creation – the Chapel of the Princes.

According to a tradition which seems to bizarrely link Medici patronage with this family's apparent aspiration to simply astonish the world with their extraordinary enterprises, the Holy Sepulchre itself was to have been dismantled and transported from Jerusalem to Florence where it was to have graced the Chapel of the Princes. It is easy to imagine the prestige the Medici family would have acquired in the Christian world with the accomplishment of such a feat. But the Granducal family seem doomed never to conclude any of their undertakings and this affliction touched the most opulent of their creations, which remained incomplete when the Medici line died out. It was only in 1962 that the decoration of the chapel was finished with the making of the inlaid marble floor of the corridor linking the two entrances, in front of the nineteenth century railing which separates the Chapel of the Princes from the choir of the church of San Lorenzo. Once more, the work was carried out by the "Opificio delle Pietre Dure" whose monogram, together with the date, is inscribed on the floor.

The New Sacristy

A narrow passage leads to the final part of the Laurentian complex. Here are displayed two marble trophies (or suits of armour) attributed to the Carrara sculptor Silvio Cosini, collaborator of Michelangelo; they were probably intended to decorate the tombs in the room which opens off the corridor – the New Sacristy. This is one of the most important spaces in the whole history of art; a work of considerable intellectual and aesthetic appeal, the New Sacristy demonstrates the fullest expression of the creative genius of Michelangelo in his capacity as architect, sculptor and poet.

The history of the New Sacristy originated with Pope Leo X's wish to dedicate a funerary chapel to his father Lorenzo "the Magnificent" and his uncle Giuliano "the Magnificent", as well as to his brother Giuliano of Nemours and his nephew Lorenzo of Urbino (the "Dukes" – the first members of the Medici family to attain noble titles). This undertaking was taken up and set into motion by Leo's successor, Pope Clement VII (formerly Cardinal Giulio de' Medici – son of Giuliano the Magnificent).

In 1520 Michelangelo was entrusted with the commission for the building of the chapel and the designing of the funerary monuments. This meant that he had to abandon work on the San Lorenzo facade project to which he had been dedicating much time and creative energy. The construction of the Sacristy spanned the years 1520 to 1534 with frequent, often dramatic, interruptions due to the turbulent history of Florence and of the Medici family itself in this period; it is enough to mention the seige of Florence in 1530. When Michelangelo left Florence definitively for Rome in 1534, the sacristy was far from complete although the sculpture was ready and the architecture more or less finished. Furthermore, Pope Clement VII had envisaged the addition of his own sepulchral monument, and that of Leo X, but the idea was never followed through. After many vicissitudes the chapel and its statues came to completion between 1554-1555, through the

The lantern of the New
Sacristy dome

patronage of Cosimo I and under the care of two of the most attentive and impassioned of Michelangelo's followers and admirers – Giorgio Vasari and Bartolommeo Ammannati.

The New Sacristy draws its inspiration from the form of Brunelleschi's Old Sacristy – a cube-shaped space surmounted by a hemispherical dome – and is, in fact, symmetrically balanced by the older chapel in the ground plan of the church. But the similarities between the two end there. In contrast to the crisp geometry of Brunelleschi we are faced here with the dynamic and allegorical power of Michelangelo. To begin with, the verticality of the structure is emphasised through the insertion of an additional storey between the walls and the dome.

The coffered vault of the dome itself (inspired by the Pantheon) expresses a dynamic liveliness through the radial accents of the coffering; this must have been accentuated by the painted decoration of Giovanni da Udine, whitewashed over in the eighteenth century.

A further impression of movement is contributed by the insertion of roundels into the pendentives; these circular forms link the dome to the great arches of the upper storey. Inserted at the top of each arch are windows of stunning originality; tapering towards the top, they have strongly projecting, curved pediments. The intermediate zone is articulated through a series of pilasters (flanking two windows on each wall) and supporting an entablature. But the most dramatically expressive part of the architecture is the lower storey. Hemmed tightly in by powerful pilasters are areas of marble architectural membering made up of blind tabernacles, more paired pilasters

The ceiling of the New Sacristy with its coffered
cupola, the grey sandstone membering and the
unusual windows which taper towards the top

View showing the *Tomb of Lorenzo, Duke of Urbino* and the marble altar

View showing the *Tomb of Giuliano, Duke of Nemours* and the group of the *Madonna and Child between Saints Cosmas and Damian*

Architectural details of the marble
areas: blind tabernacle and mask
motifs

Michelangelo
Madonna and Child and detail (on
the following pages)

Giovannangelo da Montorsoli
St. Cosmas

and decorated with swags, ribbon motifs and cornices bearing a mask motif. Here are placed the funerary monuments. The doors are situated in the narrowest areas of the walls; almost compressed by the flanking pilasters, they seem to fuse with the tabernacles above and, with their "broken" pediments, they give the impression of being subjected to enormous pressure. In a way which epitomises the univocity of Michelangelo's artistic personality the sense of tension and unease present in the architecture seems to be transferred to the sculpted figures which inhabit the Medici tombs.

According to a very early idea of Michelangelo's for the New Sacristy the tombs of Lorenzo the Magnificent (d. 1492) and that of his brother Giuliano (murdered in the

Raffaello da Montelupo
St. Damian

Pazzi conspiracy of 1478) were originally planned to form part of a free-standing, central mausoleum, also comprising the tombs of the "Dukes". The present monument to the "Magnifici" bears no effigy of either of these personalities. In fact, they are buried within a simple marble plinth; in 1559 their bodies were transferred there from the provisional tomb in the Old Sacristy. The plinth is surmounted by Michelangelo's statue of the *Madonna and Child*. This sculpture, of 1521, has been taken barely beyond the 'roughing out' stage and yet it, too, seems to be pervaded by that feeling of disquiet and pain – expressed here through the spiralling pose, the Virgin's melancholy expression and the twist with which the Christ Child turns towards his mother's breast. This statue is an

Michelangelo
Giuliano, Duke of Nemours

Michelangelo
Tomb of Giuliano, Duke of Nemours

Michelangelo
Day

intense prototype of the "serpentine" pose of which there are numerous variants in Mannerist painting and sculpture. The Madonna is flanked by the two Medici saints in attitudes of adoration: *Cosmas* (to the left) by Giovannangelo da Montorsoli and (to the right) *Damian* sculpted by Raffaello da Montelupo. Both artists were assistants to Michelangelo in the New Sacristy workshop.

On the right wall is the statue of Giuliano, Duke of Nemours (d. 1516), brother of Leo X and the third son of Lorenzo the Magnificent. He is dressed as a Captain of the Church, wearing a cuirass and holding a commander's baton and – consonant with his personification as a man of action – his head is turned sharply to the left. His facial type is common to a number of male figures sculpted by Michelangelo, in fact, when people noted that the figure did not resemble the dead Duke Michelangelo was said to have countered (with a kind of knowing artistic pride) that a few centuries on no-one would remember what Giuliano had looked like anyway.

Below the Duke, reclining on the volutes of the sarcophagus are the personifications of *Day*, a muscular male nude with his face unfinished and in shadow; and *Night* – one of the most famous figures in the history of sculpture. Michelangelo depicts her as a drowsy young woman, she lies, though, in uneasy sleep – suggested through the unstable and contorted pose. She is accompanied by symbols of the night: she wears a diadem bearing a crescent moon and a star, a barn owl perches in the cavern beneath her thigh, a bunch of poppy heads props up her foot, an empty-eyed mask – a symbol of nocturnal nightmares perhaps – leers out from beneath her arm. The marble surface is polished to a glassy smoothness (even more evident since its recent cleaning) and this makes the figure appear as if it is steeped in moonlight. It is

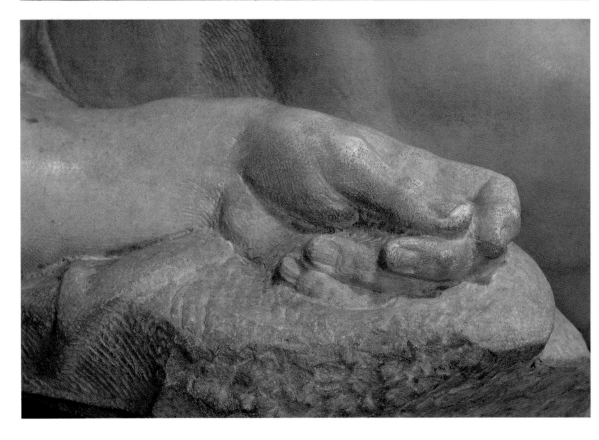

Michelangelo
Details of *Day*

Michelangelo
Night

Michelangelo
Details of *Night*

Michelangelo
Tomb of Lorenzo, Duke of Urbino

Michelangelo
Lorenzo, Duke of Urbino

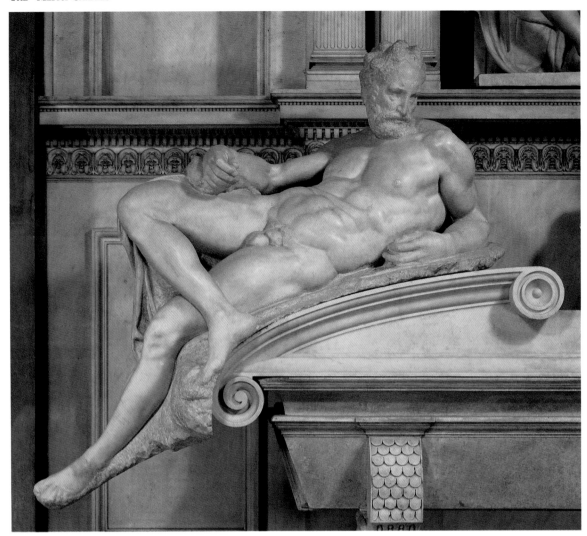

almost as if Michelangelo has here fused his strength as a sculptor with his painter's chromatic sensibilities. An inscription added by the artist to a preliminary sketch for the New Sacristy project provide us with a direct testimony of the creative ideas behind these statues:

"Day and Night speak and say: We with our swift course have brought the Duke Giuliano to death: it is only just that the Duke takes revenge as he does for this, that, as we have killed him, he, dead, has taken the light from us; and with his closed eyes has locked ours shut, which no longer shine on earth. What then would he have done with us while alive?"

Equally well known is the sonnet of Giovan Battista Strozzi which addresses itself in eulogistic tones to Michelangelo's creation:

"The Night that you see in such loveliness,
Sleeping, was carved by an angel
In this rock, and, since she sleeps, has life:
Wake her, if you disbelieve, and she will speak to you."

to which Michelangelo replied (speaking as Night) in lines full of sadness, embittered as he was by the events that had led to the fall of the Florentine Republic:

"I prize my sleep, and more my being stone,
As long as hurt and shamefulness endure.
I call it lucky not to see or hear;
So do not waken me, keep your voice down!"

On the facing wall is the tomb of Lorenzo, Duke of Urbino (d. 1519). Son of Piero the Unfortunate, Machiavelli dedicated his book *The Prince* to him. It is thought that Michelangelo's statue of the Duke was

Michelangelo
Dusk

Michelangelo
Detail of *Dusk*

Michelangelo
Dawn

sculpted in 1533. In contrast to the character and image of Giuliano, Lorenzo (who also wears a general's cuirass) is depicted as a pensive figure. In fact, he has long been known as "il Pensieroso" both in critical literature and in the context of the Neoplatonic theory of human temperament which underpins Michelangelo's depiction of the two Dukes. On the sarcophagus (which also contains the remains of Lorenzo's son, Alessandro, the first Duke of Florence) recline the figures of *Dusk* and *Dawn* (1531-1532). The latter seems to be languidly rousing herself from heavy slumber whereas *Dusk*, with his unfinished face, seems to sink slowly into sleep. Within the complex symbolism of the New Sacristy (fully explored through the ages), the concept of Time (expressed in the figures representing the four times of the day) is related to the division of human personality into the Active and the Contemplative.

The singularity of this extraordinary space and its decoration lies in the fact that it is, in effect, a complete exposition of the artistic personality of Michelangelo who expresses himself as philosopher, poet, architect and sculptor. In a sense, he also expresses himself as a painter thorugh the chromatic and lighting effects arrived at in the differing degrees of finish of his sculpted figures – from the highly polished *Night* to the roughened limbs of *Day* which give the impression of skin bronzed by the strong rays of the sun.

In front of the small choir stands a marble altar of decidedly sixteenth century style (as is the holy-water font in the right hand corner of the sacristy); the altar has its complement of brass candlesticks and two marble candelabra. The one on the left is original, made by Silvio Cosini on a design by Michelangelo, and the one to the right its copy, made by Girolamo Ticciati in 1741, after the

Michelangelo
Dawn and detail

Michelangelo
Detail of *Dawn*

Michelangelo
Detail of a bukranium
from the *Tomb of
Lorenzo, Duke of Urbino*

Michelangelo original had been accidentally smashed. A small bronze Crucifix of fine quality and thought to be by Giambologna is placed at the centre of the top step of the altar. On the walls Michelangelesque architectural drawings have been discovered beneath the plaster. Recently a marble tablet, of 1910, has been placed in the choir; this describes the statues in the Sacristy in an elegant Latin which has something of the flavour of Gabriele d'Annunzio.

From the left-hand lavabo – or vestibule – one descends to a small basement room where, in 1978, a number of charcoal drawings were discovered on the walls. Some clearly relate to specific figures by Michelangelo such as the *Eve* from the Sistine Chapel ceiling and the legs of the Giuliano of Nemours statue. The quality of the drawings is uneven and there is some uncertainty as to their attribution and the reasons for their creation. Paolo Dal Poggetto, who had the drawings restored – together with the mass of sketches, rough outlines, inscriptions and caricatures which surround them – connects them with Michelangelo's friendship with Figiovanni, the canon of San Lorenzo at the time of the work on the New Sacristy. Following the return to Florence of the Medici family after the seige of 1530, Michelangelo's friend-

Wall of the New Sacristy looking towards the altar

Sixteenth century marble altar with
candelabra designed by
Michelangelo

Detail of Michelangelesque
candelabrum

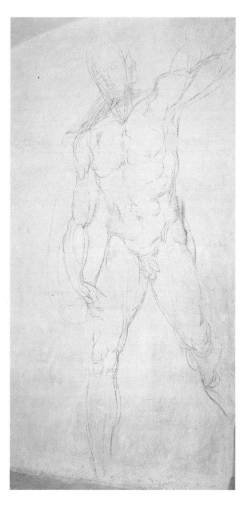

Study of allegorical figures

Standing male figure

ship with the canon held him in good stead when he needed somewhere to hide from the vengeful threats of Duke Alessandro de' Medici; this room was possibly that place of refuge. Dal Poggetto has carefully separated the clearly autograph drawings from those by Michelangelo's assistants and followers. However peripheral these unusual drawings might be to the sacristy itself, they do supply yet another facet of Michelangelo's creativity which turns this extraordinary creation of the New Sacristy of San Lorenzo into a microscosm of his artistic genius.

Study for the legs of Giuliano, Duke of Nemours

Index of artists

The index refers to the artists mentioned in the text. Numbers in bold face refer to illustrations.